THINK OUTSIDE THE BOX

PIENSA FUERA DE LA CAJA

Justine Avery & Liuba Syrotiuk

Just *think* outside the box.
Solo *piensa* fuera de la caja.

And seeing through your own personal view.

Y ver a través de tu visión particular.

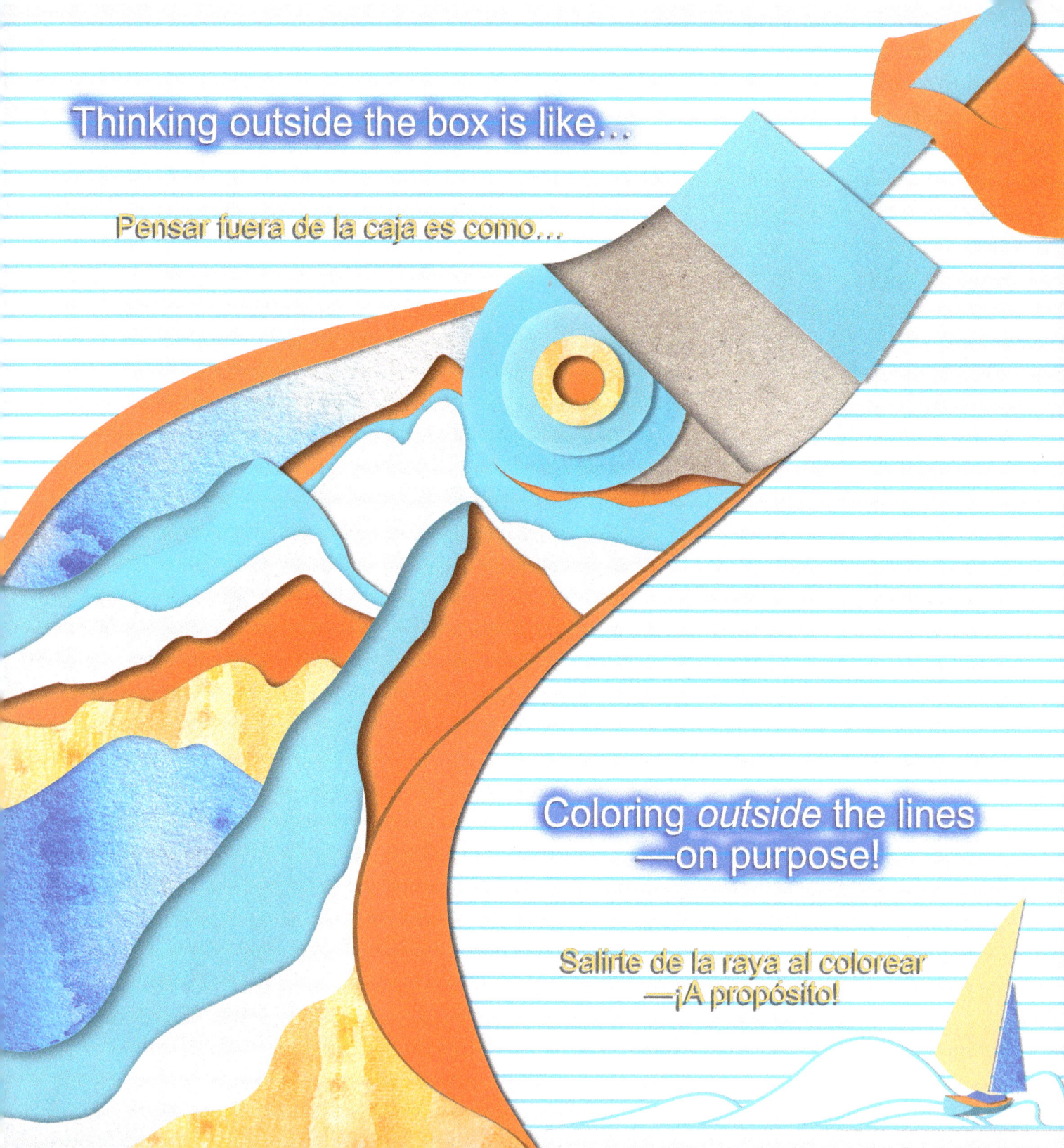

It's like trying to run a race the *slowest*.

Es como tratar de correr una carrera lo más *lento*.

It's like looking at a problem...

Es como mirar un problema...

While you're *upside down*.

Mientras estás *boca abajo*.

It's noticing the details that *no one else sees*.

Es darse cuenta de los detalles que *nadie más ve*.

It's the same as *slowing down*
—or even stopping—
when everyone else is rushing around.

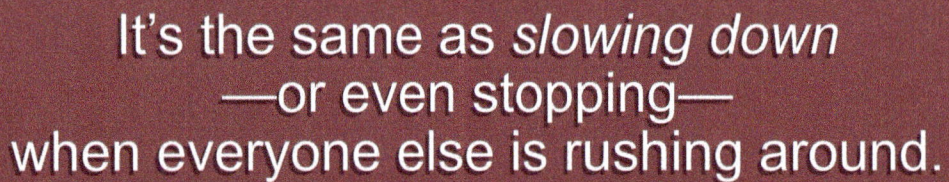

Es lo mismo que *reducir la velocidad*
—o incluso detenerse—
cuando todos los demás
están corriendo.

To everyone, everywhere...
Remember that creativity is everything.
Let yours guide you.
—J.A.

Para todos, en todas partes...
recuerda que la creatividad lo es todo.
Deja que la tuya te guíe.
—J.A.

This book is dedicated to my grandmother Nadine whose originative, positive thinking changes many lives and inspires creativity.
—L.S.

Este libro está dedicado a mi abuela Nadine, quien con su pensamiento positivo y original cambia tantas vidas e inspira a la creatividad.
—L.S.

Justine Avery is an award-winning author who loves writing stories for all sorts of readers. She was born in America but grew up-and is still growing up-all over the world as a natural explorer with a curiosity for all things. She's jumped out of airplanes, off of very high bridges, and into shark-infested waters-to name a few adventures. And books are her favorite adventures of all.

Justine Avery es una autora galardonada que ama escribir historias para todo tipo de lectores. Nació en Estados Unidos de América, pero creció, y sigue creciendo, en muchos lugares del mundo gracias a su naturaleza exploradora y a su curiosidad por todas las cosas. Justine ha brincado desde aviones, de puentes muy altos y a aguas infestadas de tiburones, por mencionar algunas de sus aventuras. Entre todas las aventuras, los libros son su aventura favorita.

Liuba Syrotiuk is a Ukrainian designer and watercolor artist. She works as an interior designer and watercolor illustrator. Liuba is a bright and sunny person, willing to find beauty in everything, especially in nature. Traveling around the world with a small box of watercolors makes her the happiest person.

Liuba Syrotiuk es una diseñadora y acuarelista ucraniana. Trabaja como diseñadora de interiores e ilustradora de acuarela. Liuba es una persona radiante y luminosa, dispuesta a encontrar la belleza en todo, especialmente en la naturaleza. Viajar alrededor del mundo con una pequeña caja de acuarelas la convierte en la persona más feliz.

FIRST BILINGUAL EDITION
Copyright © 2020 Justine Avery
Illustrated by Liuba Syrotiuk
All rights reserved.

First published 2020
by Suteki Creative

ISBN: 978-1-63882-072-7
ISBN: 978-1-63882-070-3 (ebook)
ISBN: 978-1-63882-073-4 (hardcover)
ISBN: 978-1-63882-075-8 (audio book)

In accordance with international copyright law, this publication, in full or in part, may not be scanned, copied, stored in a retrieval system, duplicated, reproduced, uploaded, transmitted, resold, or distributed online or offline—in any form or by any means—without prior, explicit permission of the author.

This bilingual Spanish-English edition first published 2021 by Suteki Creative

But *please do*... **lend this book freely!** It's *yours*—you own it. So, pass it on, trade it in, exchange it with and recommend it to other readers. Books are the very best gifts.

www.ingramcontent.com/pod-product-compliance
Lightning Source LLC
Chambersburg PA
CBHW061116070526
44583CB00027B/3310